The Mayflower Compact

by Marcia Amidon Lusted

PEBBLE
a capstone imprint

First Facts are published by Pebble
1710 Roe Crest Drive, North Mankato, Minnesota 56003.
www.mycapstone.com

Library of Congress Cataloging-in-Publication Data
Names: Lusted, Marcia Amidon, author.
Title: The Mayflower Compact / by Marcia Amidon Lusted.
Description: First edition. | North Mankato, Minnesota : Capstone Press, an imprint of Pebble, [2020]
 | Series: First facts. Shaping the United States of America | Audience: Grades K–3.
| Audience: Ages 6–8. Identifiers: LCCN 2019004129| ISBN 9781977109163 (hardcover)
| ISBN 9781977110152 (pbk.) | ISBN 9781977109187 (ebook pdf)
Subjects: LCSH: New Plymouth Colony. Mayflower Compact—Juvenile literature. | Pilgrims
(New Plymouth Colony)—Juvenile literature. | Mayflower (Ship)—Juvenile literature.
| Massachusetts—History—New Plymouth, 1620–1691—Juvenile literature.
Classification: LCC F68 .L94 2019 | DDC 974.4/02—dc23
LC record available at https://lccn.loc.gov/2019004129

Editorial Credits
Alesha Sullivan, editor; Elyse White, designer; Jo Miller, media researcher;
Katy LaVigne, production specialist

Image Credits
Library of Congress Prints and Photographs, Cover (bottom), 6, 16 (top); Newscom: akg-images, 9,
Heritage Images/The Print Collector, 13, 16, (bottom), Picture History, 7 (bottom), 10; North Wind Picture
Archives, 4, 5, 14; Shutterstock: mark renstein, 21, Michael Sean O'Leary, 7, (top), Rob Crandall, 20;
Wikimedia: Commonwealth of Massachusetts, Cover (top) 15, NARA, 19

Design Elements
Shutterstock: Scisetti Alfio

Printed and bound in China.
1671

Table of Contents

Chapter 1

A New Land

In 1620 a ship called the *Mayflower* had reached land. It had traveled for 66 days. The **Pilgrims** were on board. They had sailed from England to find a new home in North America. But they were worried. There was no king here like in England. How could they run their **colony** in this new place?

The Pilgrims prayed together on the *Mayflower* before setting sail to North America.

colony—a place that is settled by people from another country and is controlled by that country

Pilgrim—a person in the group that left England, came to North America for religious freedom, and founded Plymouth Colony in 1620

Chapter 2

Who Were the Pilgrims?

The Pilgrims left England so that they could be free to follow the religion of their choice. They landed at Plymouth Bay in 1620. They built a colony called Plymouth Plantation in present-day Massachusetts. There were 102 people on the *Mayflower*, and nearly half were Pilgrims. The others were not part of their group.

A re-creation of Plymouth Plantation shows people what the first homes of the Pilgrims may have looked like.

A Passenger's Story

William Bradford was a Pilgrim. He kept a journal during his trip to North America on the *Mayflower*. He wrote about their arrival: "Being thus passed the vast ocean, . . . they had now no friends to welcome them nor inns to entertain or refresh their weather-beaten bodies; no houses or much less towns to repair to."

7

Saints and Strangers

The Pilgrims hoped to build a church in America. They called themselves the Saints. They called the other passengers Strangers. The Strangers moved to America to become craftsmen or servants. The Saints wanted the Strangers to **worship** the way the Saints did. Because of these differences, the two groups did not get along well.

worship—to express love or honor to a higher being

A painting shows *Mayflower* passengers kneeling in prayer after coming on shore in America.

Shortly after arriving, people began to build houses in Plymouth Colony.

The new land proved to be a difficult place to live. The two groups worried about getting along. Everyone needed food and shelter. They had to work together as one group and protect each other. If there were disagreements, it would be hard to survive.

Loyalty to England

Both groups on the *Mayflower* were loyal to King James I of Great Britain. But he was far away. There was no one to **enforce** the rules here. Together, the two groups agreed to create an official list of rules. They would use it to decide how to **govern** themselves.

enforce—to make sure something happens

govern—to rule or lead

King James I (1566–1625)

13

Chapter 3

Writing the Compact

Some of the Saints wrote the list. It was called the Mayflower **Compact**. It said everyone would decide on laws together. They all agreed to follow these laws. The groups would meet together any time they needed to make a decision. Together, they would run the colony.

fted by them done (this their condition considered) might
be as firme as any patent; and in some respects more sure.

The forme was as follo:

In ÿ name of god Amen. We whose names are underwritten,
the loyall subiects of our dread soueraigne Lord King Iames,
by ÿ grace of god, of great Britaine, franc, & Ireland king,
defendor of ÿ faith, &c.

Haueing vndertaken, for ÿ glorie of god, and aduancemente
of ÿ christian faith, and honour of our king & countrie, a voyage to
plant ÿ first Colonie in ÿ Northerne parts of Virginia. doe
by these presents solemnly & mutualy in ÿ presence of god, and
one of another, couenant, & combine our selues togeather into a
Ciuill body politick; for our beter ordering, & preseruation & fur=
theranco of ÿ ends aforesaid; and by vertue hearof to Enacte,
constitute, and frame shuch just & equall Lawes, ordinances,
Acts, constitutions, & offices, from time to time, as shall be thought
most meete & convenient for ÿ generall good of ÿ Colonie: vnto
which we promise all due submission and obedience. In witnes
wherof we haue hereunder subscribed our names at Cap=

compact—an agreement or contract between people or groups

The men on the ship signed the compact, agreeing to its rules.

Religious Differences

A Pilgrim leader named William Brewster wrote most of the compact. He helped form a **Separatist** church in England before coming to America. Many Separatists left their homes because they disagreed with the Church of England. They wanted to practice their own religion. Brewster continued to work for the Separatist church throughout his life at Plymouth Plantation.

The Signers

On November 11, 1620, 41 men signed the Mayflower Compact. Women were not allowed to sign. By signing the document, the Saints and Strangers created the first **democracy** in America. The land would one day be known as the United States.

democracy—a kind of government in which the people make decisions by voting

Separatist—one of a group of British people who wanted to practice religion separately from the Church of England

Chapter 4

Foundation for the Future

The Mayflower Compact didn't just help the Pilgrims. The agreement later helped build the **foundation** for the United States. The men who wrote the U.S. **Constitution** more than 100 years later thought about the compact. Then they wrote rules for how the country would be run, similar to the Pilgrims. They said that the people would choose their leaders and help make the laws.

We the People of the United States, in order to form a more perfect Union, establish justice, ensure domestic Tranquility, provide for the common defence, promote the general Welfare, and secure the Blessings of Liberty to ourselves and our Posterity, do ordain and establish this Constitution for the United States of America.

Article. I.

Section. 1. All legislative Powers herein granted shall be vested in a Congress of the United States, which shall consist of a Senate and House of Representatives.

Section. 2. The House of Representatives shall be composed of Members chosen...

constitution—a written system of laws in a country that state the rights of people and the powers of government

foundation—a base on which something rests or is built

The present-day United States shares similarities to the Pilgrims' colony. We still have a democracy. We vote. We choose leaders to help run our country. The Mayflower Compact was written hundreds of years ago. But it is still an important piece of our country today.

People vote on Election Day to choose new leaders for the United States.

Leaders gather in Washington, D.C., to work for the people of the United States of America.

colony (KAH-luh-nee)—an area that has been settled by people from another country, typically ruled by another country

compact (KAHM-pakt)—an agreement or contract between people or groups

constitution (kahn-stuh-TOO-shuhn)—a written system of laws in a country that state the rights of people and the powers of government

democracy (di-MAH-kruh-see)—a kind of government in which the people make decisions by voting

enforce (in-FORS)—to make sure something happens

foundation (foun-DAY-shuhn)—a base on which something rests or is built

freedom (FREE-duhm)—the right to do and say what you like

govern (GUHV-urn)—to rule or lead

Pilgrim (PIL-gruhm)—a person in the group that left England, came to North America for religious freedom, and founded Plymouth Colony in 1620

Separatist (SEP-uh-rah-tist)—one of a group of British people who wanted to practice religion separately from the Church of England

worship (WUR-ship)—to express love or honor to a higher being

Read More

Honders, Christine. *Mayflower Compact*. Documents of American Democracy. New York: PowerKids Press, 2017.

Son, John. *If You Were a Kid on the Mayflower*. New York: Scholastic, 2018.

Troupe, Thomas Kingsley. *The Pilgrims' Voyage to America: A Fly on the Wall History*. North Mankato, MN: Picture Window Books, 2017.

Internet Sites

Pilgrim Hall Museum: Text of the Mayflower Compact
www.pilgrimhallmuseum.org/mayflower_compact_text.htm

Plimoth Plantation: Mayflower and Mayflower Compact
www.plimoth.org/learn/just-kids/homework-help/mayflower-and-mayflower-compact

Critical Thinking Questions

1. What do you think might have happened if the Pilgrims did not write the Mayflower Compact?

2. In your own words, describe what a compact is. Use the text on page 14 and the glossary to help you.

3. Would you leave your home for a new, unknown land if it gave you more freedom to live the way you wanted to? Why or why not?

Index